Yoruba Mythology

Orisha Gods and Goddesses of West Africa

Preface

Delve into the world of Yoruba mythology!

Do you want to learn about an ancient religion still practiced today?

Have you heard of Orisha and IFA and want to know more about them?

Then you've chosen the right book.

The Yoruba people have existed for centuries and can still be found today across parts of Africa, practicing their religion and worshipping their gods and goddesses, collectively known as the Orisha.

This book will give you an in-depth look at African spiritual practice, the Ifa, the Orishas, and more. It's an easy-to-read guide that will tell you all you need to know, provided you can keep an open mind.

Table of Contents

Introduction

Who are the Yoruba?

They are one of the three primary ethnic groups in Southwestern Nigeria, with smaller groups in Northeastern Togo, the Ivory Coast, Ghana, and Benin. They are not a small group, with at least 30 million members, and are considered one of the biggest West African tribes.

Like almost every culture in the world, Yoruba culture is steeped in poetry, allegories, mythology, and knowledge of the Ifa divination system. These practices are a constant reminder to the people of their practices and their long and colorful history, handed down through the generations via oral tradition, which has shaped who they are today.

Yoruba mythology is littered with spirits and gods, otherwise known as orishas, and the primary, supreme being. The orishas are male and female, and it's unclear how many there are – at least 400, although some sources say there are so many it's impossible to count them.

Tradition tells us that the Orisha are ghosts sent by the supreme being to help humans, teaching them everything they need to know spiritually. Most are thought to reincarnate themselves as humans, living ordinary lives but with tremendous power and intelligence. However, some believe they were ordinary folk who were deified on their deaths because of how they lived spiritually and physically.

It's clear to all that the Yoruba people revere their gods and ancestors, even though only oral records exist of their history. However, most anthropologists struggle to agree on whether the lineage rites are religious or purely out of courtesy. Some communities believe their ancestors became demigods when they died, but they had to take on a real deity's persona first. This is much the same as possession, a Yoruba faith form where a medium takes on the trait of at least one god or goddess.

The pages of this book are packed with interesting, useful information on who the Yoruba people are, how they practice, and the Orishas they worship.

Chapter 1:

Understanding Spiritual Practices in Africa

The Yoruba people in West Africa are thought to be the first to practice belief in the Orishas, as far back as 500 to 300 BCE. These practices and beliefs made their way to the Caribbean, the Americas, and other places when the transatlantic slave trade began. People in these places began incorporating the Yoruba religion into other diaspora religions, like Santería and Voodoo.

Most of what we know about the Orishas, including rituals and stories, has only ever existed in oral form, which makes it hard to know what's right and what isn't. However, most of the stories do share some common aspects.

Ifa – Yoruba Religion

The Yoruba people follow a religion known as Ifa, which is largely prevalent across Southwestern Nigeria, particularly in the following states:

- Benin
- Ekiti
- Kogi
- Kwara
- Lagos
- Ogun
- Ondo
- Osun
- Oyo
- Togo

Ifa can be dated a long way back, which means it has long been ingrained in Yoruba life, leading to the practices and beliefs that began migrating across the world during the slave trade years.

The enslaved Yoruba people began sharing Ifa with other enslaved African people sent to the Caribbean and Americas. These people would eventually get involved with other religions, intermingling Ifa with them to create new versions, including:

- Candomblé
- Haitian Vodou
- Santería
- Trinidad orisha
- Umbanda

- Voodoo

During the 16th to 18th centuries, Ifa even crossed with some parts of Christianity, especially Catholicism. Key parts of Ifa include the following:

Olodumare

One of the most important parts of the diaspora religions is Olodumare and his other aspects – Olofi and Olorun. It is firmly believed that Olodumare created the Universe and is the sole source of all energy. Ifa, Santería, and Voodoo revere Olodumare as the ultimate being who holds all the power and knowledge. Directly or indirectly, everything is connected to Olodumare, and practitioners carry out their venerations and actions in his name.

Aṣẹ

Aṣẹ is considered the life force, integrated into everything, living or otherwise, and is said to contain two types of power:

- Spiritual power
- The power to launch events and actions within the physical world

Whatever happens, be it a conversation, a prayer, a song, or even a curse, it is down to Aṣẹ. Aṣẹ is in everything, from humans and animals to water, grass, trees, stone, and even the Yoruba pantheon gods and ancestors; it is one of the most important parts of the Yoruba religion. Olodumare grants Aṣẹ the energy, while his Olurun aspect grants the power, allowing Aṣẹ to be the ruler of heaven. Aṣẹ is also associated with the sun, allowing the existence of all life forms.

Orún

Orún exists on a plane far higher than the physical world and is an invisible realm. Olodumare dwells within Orún, and it is also where the Orishas originated. All life begins here before it takes on a physical form on Earth, in a similar belief to the following:

- **Christianity** – heaven
- **Norse Mythology** – Valhalla and Fólkvangr
- **Roman and Greek** – Elysian Fields (Elysium)

Olurun presides over Orún.

Ayé

The Yoruba people consider the physical world to be Ayé. This is Earth, where humans, animals, and plant life live and die – anything that exists within the natural world's ecosystem. Ayé is permeated throughout with Aṣẹ, allowing Orishas to travel as they wish between

Orún and Ayé. It was brought into being through Olodumare's will, with the help of the early Orishas, and no matter what happens in Ayé, another aspect of Olodumare, called Olofi, oversees it.

Ori

Ifa practitioners firmly believe that all humans' heads are filled with their ori, better known as their souls, essence, or spirit. The ori has a special journey. When it is created, it is sent to Olodumare, who imbues it with the personality, characteristics, and traits it needs. The ori is then connected to a specific Orisha and sent to the physical world to inhabit a person. The Orisha is carefully chosen to help guide the person through their life and influence their direction. Perhaps the most important aspect of this is that because the ori is said to reside in the head, the Yoruba people see that part of the body as significant.

Iponri

Described as a "higher state of consciousness," the iponri is what we, as humans, strive to reach as our ultimate goal. It is also said that iponri correlates to the ori in Orún. If you can recognize your destiny, it is said that the connection between you and your iponri will open fully, allowing you to access the Orishas' knowledge and wisdom. When you die, your iponri and ori are reunited in the afterlife, forming an egun. Some practitioners firmly believe in reincarnation, saying that, in some cases, a person may come back within their bloodline. When this happens, the iponri and ori break apart once more.

Ebo

Ebo is significant in Ifa as it is considered to be a concept relating to making ritual sacrifices to the Orishas. Ebo is only done in a religious context, typically during Ifa divination. Practitioners typically do it when they are calling on a divine being to provide their guidance and power, and it is considered a sign of respect, proving you are intent upon keeping the balance between the heavens and the Earth intact. It also indicates that you call upon the divine beings to ask for their wisdom to discover your destiny. Finding the right sacrifice is important as it shows you as a true believer and indicates you truly want to learn everything about the Orishas so you can put your knowledge into practice.

The most common sacrifices are animals because the Orishas can benefit from each part:

- **The vital organs and blood** – full of life essence, which is said to help the Orishas feed their own energies
- **The meat** – provides sustenance, which is said to boost the Orishas' physical strength
- **The head** – this is the most significant part of the animal, which contains the divine power given to the animal at birth by Olodumare.

Animals may not be as powerful as humans, but as living things, the Supreme Being's power touches them; thus, they contain his essence.

Practitioners can also use inanimate objects during their rituals, but whatever they choose, it must have a strong association with their Orisha. These will typically reflect the Orisha's favorite food or symbol – more about these later. These objects contain energy that is absorbed and transformed into the power the Orisha needs for sustenance. In the ritual, the practitioners use prayer to give their sacrificial items power, allowing the Orisha to channel the resulting energy deep within themselves. While these are just as powerful as using animals for sacrifices, it does take longer to get right.

The Creation Myth

The Yoruba religion tells us that Olodumare was solely responsible for creating the Universe. However, the Orishas traveled the Universe looking for inhabitable planets, and when they came across the Earth, they said it was far too wet and no one could live there. After a while, an Orisha called Obatala returned to Earth and decided to change it so that humans could live there. Using winged beasts, a mollusk with special soil, and a cloth-like material, he created some landforms. The soil was added to water and spread across the planet by the winged beasts, thus forming the Earth's crust. As the beasts beat their wings, the soil spread out, but it was uneven and formed valleys, hills, and mountains.

While Obatala was doing his work, Olodumare went to the outer reaches of space, collecting cosmic matter and gasses and forming them into a celestial body shaped like an orb. He used his powers to force the orb to erupt, forming a gigantic ball of fire, and he placed it near Earth. That orb was the sun, and its heat and light began to dry out the lands, setting them into solid ground. The sun also provided the light needed for people to see when part of Earth was not facing it. Olodumare also decided to provide an Orisha called

Yemoja with a gift. Yemoja is considered every Orishas's mother, so he created the moon for her. The moon would reflect light from the sun onto the part of the planet not facing the sun, thus allowing a silvery glow to keep the Earth lit up and not in complete darkness.

Now the land was set firm among the waters known as the seas, Obatala looked for a place to settle. He found his place on higher ground and named it Ile-Ife. It became a fertile place, with bushes, trees, grass, and flowers growing through rich soil in a bid to reach the sun's light and heat. Obatala decided that the Earth could support human life and began to use mud and clay to form figures. These were baked hard by the sun and given life by Olodumare, each given consciousness. The Yoruba people called Ile-Ife by another name – Ife Oodaye – which translates to "cradle of existence."

The Link between Yoruba, Christianity, and Islam

Throughout the 14th century, the Yoruba people traded with nomadic Malian Soninke merchants called the Wangara. Their trade led to Islam integrating with the Yoruba culture, soon becoming a strong part of their religion. Between the 17th and 19th centuries, many mosques were constructed. By the time the Yoruba people were sent as enslaved people to the Americas, many of them had fully integrated Islam into their religion or converted to it.

In the 19th century, the Yoruba people began learning of Christianity and other Western ideas when European missionaries arrived with the traders who set up commercial businesses with the local people. These missionaries began to spread the word of Christianity, sometimes using syncretism to relate Yoruba stories and pantheon members to their counterparts in Christianity. Olodumare and Olorun were identified as the Abrahamic god, and Yemoja as the Virgin Mary. The British and French colonizers were definitely more successful in converting Yoruba people – the British pushed Protestantism, and the French pushed Roman Catholicism.

The Yoruba religion began merging with these, creating new worship forms. This resulted in Ifa becoming even more divided; it had already split into sects that differed in practice and rituals. Churches were constructed for people to worship, despite the Yoruba religion not having a dedicated place of worship for ceremonies and prayers. During the 1970s, the Yoruba people of Southwestern Nigeria created their own religion and named it Nigerian Chrislam, a merger of Christianity and Islam which also retained aspects of diaspora religions; despite this, many of the Yoruba people from these areas stayed as Muslims, while Christians remained in the minority.

The Egúns

Egún translates to "ancestors" or "bones." The double meaning is used by Yoruba people to connect the bones in their bodies to their ancestors, thus emphasizing a definite connection between the living and ancestors. They are split into categories based on relationships with humans. Those categories are:

- **Egún Lya/Egún Baba:** the egún belonging to the immediate family of their connected person, such as siblings or parents.
- **Egún Idlile:** the egún belonging to hereditary ancestors and blood relatives
- **Egún iLu:** the egún belonging to those who founded the person's clan, town, community, etc.
- **Egún Eleko:** these egún are friends of those you may have met in another life
- **Abiku:** the egún belonging to stillbirth babies

or those who died not long after birth

- **Egún Enia Sasa:** the egún of accomplished or famous people, like the great priestesses and priests
- **Oso:** the egún belonging to medicine men/women and indigenous warlords
- **Olufe:** the egún belonging to the high priests or Babalawos
- **Eleye/Aja:** the egún belonging to witches
- **Ebora:** the egún representing lava and fire
- **Egún Igi:** the egún inhabiting the world's sacred trees

The Egún is also split into categories related to cultural stereotypes; each has its own characteristics, benefits, colors, abilities, and dangers. Those categories are:

Africanos y Congos

Perhaps better known as Africans and Congo, these egún belonged to the royals of Africa, including the kings and queens, who were enslaved and sent to the Americas. They are used to help defend against those who mean to do harm using the occult.

- **Offerings:** cigars, tobacco, okra, coffee, corn meal, rum

- **Colors:** orange, black, purple, brown

Orientales

Best known as Asians, these egún came from India, China, Korea, Japan, and other Asian countries. They are said to bring luck in love and with money and are used to help people improve their businesses and financial standing.

- **Offerings:** citrus fruits, incense
- **Colors:** pink, red

Haitianos

Best known as Haitian, these egún came from Haiti and are used to encourage friendliness, hospitality, and respect for elders and family.

- **Offerings:** sweet potato pudding, pumpkin and beef soup, bitter oranges, cocoa
- **Colors:** orange, red, blue

Indios

Otherwise known as Native Americans, these egún are used to help a person seek knowledge and wisdom, help provide patience, aid spiritual warfare, and help in judicial matters.

- **Offerings:** Tobacco, corn meal, black coffee

- **Colors:** blue, yellow

Arabes

Better known as Arabs, these egún are used to help and assist with magical forces, significantly, the djinn.

- **Offerings:** oil, garbanzo beans, garlic, flatbread
- **Colors:** green, black

Gitanos y Gitanes

Otherwise known as gypsies, these egún are said to help with romance, passion, palmistry, fortune telling, and divination.

- **Offerings:** cigarettes, Aguardiente liquor, crystals, and tarot cards
- **Colors:** black, red

Santos

These egún belong to the saints, hence Santos, mostly those who practice Roman Catholicism. Every saint has distinct protections and attributes; for example, Saint Jude, the patron saint of lost causes, and Saint Christopher, best known as a protector against sudden death.

- **Offerings:** iconography and other things associated with certain saints
- **Colors:** every saint has a specific color

Angeles

These egún belong to the guardian angels. There are many of them, each having their own characteristics and attributes; for example, the Angel Gabriel, protector of the military and messengers, and the Angel Nuriel, who provides protection against hailstorms.

- **Offerings:** None – guardian angels have no need of them
- **Colors:** angels are translucent, which means they are connected to every color on the spectrum

Médicas/Curandera/Santiguadores

These egún belong to doctors, healers, and faith healers. They are used to help in all kinds of medical matters, finding cures for diseases and illnesses, recovery, herbalism, medicine, and faith healing.

- **Offerings:** candles, herbal teas, religious apparatus
- **Colors:** white, yellow

Heroes y Liders

These egún belong to heroes and leaders who fight in battles and wars, figuratively and literally speaking.

- **Offerings:** weapons, cigars, alcohol

- **Colors:** white

Chamanes, Yerbateros, Brujos y Trabajadores Espirituales

These belong to shamans, herbalists, witches, and spiritualists, respectively. They help with matters related to visions, magic, healing, omens, and herbalism.

- **Offerings:** liquor, black coffee (unsweetened), cigars
- **Colors:** green, brown

Escalvos

These egún belong to enslaved people who have died and are used to help people overcome obstacles and help with hard work and patience.

- **Offerings:** Corn meal, cigars, okra, coffee
- **Colors:** white, people

Infantiles

These egún belong to stillborn babies or children who died as infants. They may often manifest themselves as those who play tricks on humans but are also incredibly protective of whomever they are connected to.

- **Offerings:** coins, candy, sweets, toys
- **Colors:** yellow, orange

Ánima Benditas y Anima Solas

These egún belong to the souls of the blessed and lost, the spirits heading to purgatory or heaven. They are used to help in almost anything while they are bound to Earth, provided the person asking for help prays to them and provides light they can follow to get to them.

- **Offerings:** ice cubes, holy water, liquor, drinks
- **Colors:** black, red

Libertadores

The egún of liberators, they help people study and learn, and aid in court cases and gaining freedom.

- **Offerings:** brandy, cigars
- **Colors:** white, yellow

Vagabundos y Bohemios

These egún provide help to writers, musicians, and artists of all kinds. They provide inspiration for drawing, playing musical instruments, songwriting, drawing, short stories, novels, poetry, letters, and singing.

- **Offerings:** bread, toast, crackers
- **Colors:** brown, green

Elementales

These egún belong to the elements – earth, air, water, and fire - the four cardinal directions – north, east, south, west – and the four winds – Notus, Boreas, Zephyrus, Eurus.

- **Offerings:** items related to cardinal directions or elements, depending on what you are asking for
- **Colors:** White (air, south), Red (fire, north), Brown (earth), Yellow (east), Blue (water), Black (west)

Pirates y Marineros

Belonging to pirates and mariners, these egún bring strength, courage, fearlessness, and the ability to overcome adversity in life.

- **Offerings:** rum, sugarcane, cigars
- **Colors:** red, black, white

Chapter 2:

The Orishas and the IFA

The Orishas are one of the most important parts of the diaspora religions, including Ifa. In fact, Ifa's belief system is considerable, and they consistently maintain that there are "400+1" Orishas, which is how they say there are too many to count. A pantheon also exists where the most influential Orishas are included, but this is nowhere near the number of those that truly exist.

The Orishas

So, what or who are the Orishas? They are supernatural beings often known as deities or divine spirits. They also act as channels, allowing the Supreme Being contact and communication with humans.

Many diaspora religions have created their own versions of the pantheon, including the Orishas important to them. However, some Orishas are shared by all the different belief systems, and these are normally thought of as the Chief Beings.

The Orishas within the pantheon are split into two groups – cool Orishas (known as gbigona) and hot Orishas (known as tutu.) The hot Orisha are fearless and strong and can easily be upset – hot-tempered if you like. Conversely, the cool Orisha are agreeable, peaceful, and tranquil. The next chapter will look at which Orishas fall into each category, and you'll see that they each have their own foods, colors, symbols, and associated items.

Categories

The Orishas are also separated into three other categories:

- The Orishas who were there at the creation
- Those who came into existence after
- Those who epitomized natural forces

Some of the Orishas were mortal to start with, deification giving them a place with the gods. Others epitomize the four elements – air, fire, earth, and water. The diaspora religions don't consider god and evil in the same way Christian religions do; while they do have links between some Orishas and saints or angels, they don't consider any of them to be completely evil or completely good. Each Orisha has negative and positive qualities.

The Core Pantheon

The core pantheon is where you will find the most important Orishas. You will learn more about them later, but here's some basic information to get you started:

- **Babalu-Aye**: an Earth spirit
- **Eshu**: the chief enforcer for the Orishas and one of the original deities
- **Iya Nla**: the source of creation and another original Orisha
- **Nana Buluku**: mother of the moon, the stars, and the sun
- **Obatala**: the Orisha who created humanity, the Sky Father
- **Oduduwa**: founded Ile-Ife and was one of the Yoruba people's divine gods
- **Ogun**: metalworker and warrior
- **Olokun**: the Orisha for all water.
- **Ori**: personifies the life essence
- **Orunmila**: provides a channel between the Orishas, Olodumare, and humans
- **Osanyin**: the Orisha of herbalists and healers
- **Oshosi**: the Orisha for nature and animals
- **Oshumare**: the Orisha for rainbows.

- **Oshun**: a mortal deified into an Orisha and one of the river deities
- **Otin**: a legendary Orisha, Otin protects the Otin River and is a warrior
- **Oya**: the Orisha for rebirth and death
- **Shango**: one of the Yoruba royal ancestors, a mortal deified to become an Orisha
- **Yemoja**: mother of all Orishas and an important water spirit

The Extended Pantheon

The remainder contains plenty of other Orishas, and talking about all of them would take up far too much time. So, these are the more popular ones:

- **Aganju**: Aganju was a mortal initially and was considered Shango's brother or father. He ruled the Oyo Empire for a while as Shango did, but he is connected to fire, whereas Shango is connected to lightning and thunder.
- **Ajaka**: Ajaka also ruled the Oyo Empire but for two different periods. His first reign saw him thought of as weak because he allowed his warriors to have way more freedom than typically allowed. His people overthrew him. When

Shango died, Ajaka took the throne again, ruling as forcefully as Shango. Because he was so loved, he was deified into an Orisha when he died.

- **Ara**: Ara personifies thunder, but Shango usually overshadows him in the pantheon. Isolated areas in Nigeria venerate Ara, but he has never been as widely worshipped as many of the other Orishas. He was thought to have been included in the core pantheon for all Yoruba people, but he was pushed out after Shango's death and deification.

- **Ayangalu**: The patron saint of drummers, Ayangalu started as a mortal and was considered the first drummer. On his death, deification made him an Orisha. He has long been seen as a musician's muse, specifically drummers, and helps inspire their creativity. In the 20th century, the rise of popular music saw drumming gain significant popularity, and Ayangalu was considered even more important to the community.

- **Egungun**: Egungun is the patron saint of the dead. Festivals called Odun Egungun are celebrated in his honor, and attendants dress in masks and opulent costumes disguised as egun or Orishas. The festival is a chance for them to pay homage to the revered dead and their ancestors. The festival involves "layering," whereby attendants wear several layers of clothing, each representing one egun or Orisha, allowing quick costume changes throughout the performances.

- **Erinle**: The Orisha of farming, hunting, and herbalism, Erinle was mortal and was well-known as an excellent hunter. He was also known for keeping the town of Ilobu safe when the Fulani invaded. One local tradition says that when he went hunting one day, he sank into the ground outside Ilobu and became the Erinle River. On his death, he was deified, and Yoruba people everywhere now revere him.

- **Ibeji**: They are the patron saint of twins and are gender fluid. Twins are considered magical in Yoruba culture and are thought to be protected by Ibeji and Shango. Twins are commonly considered spiritually connected to one another, so it is considered bad luck when one dies. Parents can try to offset this by having a representation of the dead twin carved by a Babalawo. The parents then treat this carving as a real twin and care for it as such. The connection with the living twin goes into the carving, inhabited by the dead twin's spirit, and thus they keep their magical powers.

- **Iroko**: Iroko personifies the Iroko trees found on Africa's west coast. Iroko are hardwood trees; they can survive for upwards of 500 years and are thought to offer healing properties. The trees are protected by the Orisha Iroko, and when those trees are used for healing, his power is invoked. However, legend has it that if you are looking at an Iroko tree and see the Orisha, you are not long for this world. When an Iroko tree is chopped down, it must be accompanied by a prayer to its spirit.

- **Logun Ede**: The Logun Ede are among the most unique Orishas because their characteristics are feminine and masculine – they are female for six months of the year and male for the other six months. During their female phase, they reside in rivers and freshwater lakes; during their male phase, they live in the forests.

- **Moremi**: Moremi was legendary among the Yoruba people, their queen and a heroine who helped free the Ile-Ife kingdom from the Ugbo kingdom. She was married to Oranmiyan, Oduduwa's son, and she displayed her courage and strength by allowing the Ugbo to take her captive in exchange for freeing her people with their lives intact. The king of Ugbo fell for her beauty and married her, making her the queen of Ugbo. This allowed her to learn everything about them, including their secrets, and when she escaped, she told her people everything she had learned. This allowed the Yoruba to defeat Ugbo and Moremi to enter the Orishas pantheon on her death.

- **Oba**: The patron of the River Oba, she was Shango's first wife. Oshun, his second wife, tricked Oba into cutting her own ear off and trying to get her husband to eat it. When Shango learned what had happened, he exiled his Oba. Because of this, the Rivers Oba and Osun meet at a point where the rapids are turbulent and angry. While she was in exile, Oba made sure to protect the people of Iwo, earning her deification on her death.

- **Oko**: The patron saint of farmers and hunters, Oka protects people from sorcery and is considered one of the most important parts of the African harvest festival, held every year when the white yam crop is brought in. While he and Shango were close, Oko married Oya, one of Shango's wives, and Yemoja. Many people believe that the bees are Oko's messengers, taking messages between him and the other Orishas.

- **Olumo**: The city of Abeokuta is found in the State of Ogun in Nigeria, and Olumo is its patron saint. Near Abeokuta is a natural fortress called Olumo Rock, a fortress used in the 19th century during the inter-tribal war. He is associated with stone and earth, and those living in Abeokuta still believe he is their protector to this day.

- **Oranyan**: While Oduduwa was still alive, his grandson Oranyan was heir to Ile-Ife's throne. When Oduduwa died, he was deified and became an Orisha, and Oranyan was crowned king. It is said that he founded Oyo-Ile, which later became the Oyo Empire. His wife, Erinmwide of Egor, birthed a son who later became the God

King of Benin, Eweka I, and their descendants are still ruling the kingdom now. On his death, Oranyan was also deified as an Orisha.

- **Orò**: Orò is the patron saint of bullroarers, which are musical instruments used in rituals and for justice. Every year a patriarchal festive honors him, but only the males descending from the native parents can attend – foreigners and females must stay inside until the festival ends; it is blasphemy for any female or foreigner to lay eyes on Orò. Special festivals are often included in the mourning period for monarchs.

- **Oronsen**: Owo is a government area in the State of Ondo, Nigeria, and Oronsen is its patron. It can be traced back to Ile-Ife, which Oduduwa's sons founded. Orensen entered politics after meeting King Rerengejen on a hunting trip and was brought into his harem. She later told the king that she was an Orisha but was satisfied as his wife; she only asked that he and the rest of his wives not break her taboos – three unbreakable ones. However, jealousy caused his other wives to break them when he was away hunting, and Orensen fled. Before she died, she told the king she would watch over Owo forever if he held a remembrance festival to honor her.

- **Yewa**: The patron of the Yewa River, Yewa is said to protect sand miners, fishermen, loggers, and crabbers. The blue crab is one of the most popular food sources from the river, and it is said that Yewa is strongly associated with it.

The Ajogun

We can't talk about Orishas without mentioning the Ajogun. These personify the malevolent forces and evil spirits that plague the Orishas and humanity; there are too many to count. That said, it is believed eight warlords lead the Ajogun, each the personification of a negative concept:

- **Àrùn: The Ajogun of Disease**. Àrùn is mostly depicted as an elderly shaman with a staff member of a night adder. When he walks, the earth turns to ash, and any plants or trees he touches die. If a healthy animal suddenly dies and its body rots quickly, Àrùn is thought to be near.
- **Ẹgbà: The Ajogun of Paralysis**. It is said that Ẹgbà has interfered when a person has sleep paralysis, and some who have it say they have seen

an evil, dark figure from the corner of their eyes. Some say he can get into your dreams and cause horrifying nightmares.

- **Èpè: The Ajogun of Curses**. Usually depicted as a thin man, Èpè is said to wear tattered clothing and carry an old, crooked walking stick. The stick has an eye on it that can move about as it wants, and if anyone gazes upon the eye, it is said they will be cursed.

- **Èṣe: The Ajogun of Affliction**. Èṣe carries a two-sided sword, each side representing a different type of affliction – one side mental and the other physical. He has different length legs and has a bad limp as he shuffles along with the axe dragging along behind him. When he enters his victims' homes, he can be heard as the finger bones on his necklace rattle.

- **Èwọ̀n: The Ajogun of Imprisonment**. Èwọ̀n takes great delight in imprisoning people and torturing them in horrific ways but not allowing them to die. He has hot pokers for fingers, and he uses them to jab the flesh of his victims. His pet is Ilozumba, a red-necked buzzard who pecks the eyes of Èwọ̀n's victims.

- **Ikú: The Ajogun of Death**. Typically thought of as the warlord's chief, Ikú carries a huge spear with a shaft carved from the spine of an element and a blackened iron head. His necklace bears his victims' skulls, and he normally has an African wild dog with him called Ahwinahwi.

- **Òfò: The Ajogun of Loss**. When Òfò arrives, the air becomes heavy, causing breathing difficulties, and the weather is stormy and dark. When someone has depression, it is thought to be caused by Òfò when he grabs the heart of a person who loses a loved one and does not let go.

- **Ọràn: The Ajogun of Trouble and Problems**. As a shapeshifter, Ọràn can take on any form he wants. Often, he will become a person who is not at home, wreak havoc on their relationships and lives, and then disappears before they come home.

The Ifa Divination System

The diaspora religions firmly believe that all humans contain the Orishas' power, but more so in their heads than anywhere else. This is a merger between the divine and the mortal in the human essence, a place where the spirit and the consciousness reside, and it means that we can all access the Orishas' supernatural power. This is an important factor in the Ifa divination system because divination is only made possible when this connection is exploited.

The Yoruba people practice Ifa divination widely, using religious writings and mathematical formulae. The corpus is huge and is called the Odu Ifa. It has 256 odus (parts), and these are divided into ese (verses). There are about 800 eses in each odu, and each has a divination signature of its own, determined by a Babalawo. The Babalawo determines the signature using sacred palm nuts and a divination chain.

It is undoubtedly one of the most ancient religious practices worldwide and has existed for at least 8000 years. The Yoruba people's ancestors developed it in West Africa in the Cradle of Civilization, and some say it was the influence behind every religion in the world. Ifa had become the predominant religion for the Yoruba people by the 8th century.

The Rules of Ifa

While there are many more rules, these are the primary ones that all practitioners must live by:

1. Only one Supreme Being exists
2. There isn't a supreme evil being
3. Apart from two days, your life is not foretold, and everything can be changed. Those two days are your birth and death days
4. From the moment of your birth, you have the right to success, happiness, and fulfillment
5. Your primary life goal is to grow as a person, learning along the way
6. Your blood relatives help preserve your essence
7. Earth is not a home; it is a marketplace. Heaven is your home
8. You constantly transition between Earth and heaven
9. You are literally, not figuratively, physically part of the universe
10. You must not harm anyone deliberately
11. You must not harm the environment deliberately
12. Your spiritual and physical sides must work together
13. Before you are born, your life path is set, whether you can see it or not. Your life goal is to stay on it – divination provides the map you need to do this

14. Your ancestors' spirits are real, and you must honor them
15. Success is always guaranteed when you make sacrifices for the greater good
16. The Orishas' power lives in you
17. You must fear nothing in your life.

Chapter 3:

The Cool Orishas

These Orishas are often called the tutu Orishas and are cool-tempered. Their characteristics are a patient nature, gentleness, and a calm aura, and their associated color is white. They are said to be helpful Orishas.

Orunmila

The Orisha of wisdom, knowledge, and divination, especially Ifa divination, Orunmila is also the Ifa Oracle's patron. Practitioners invoke his name in rituals where the priestesses and priests practice divination. There is a belief that life has a duality – males only exist because of female essence, and vice versa.

Many believe Orunmila witnessed fate and creation, second only to Olodumare, the Orisha responsible for all creation. He is well-versed in every divine and mortal matter, with unfailing wisdom. Orunmila is also said to be one of the original Orishas, created by

Olodumare, rather than being a mortal who was deified into one. Because of this, his place in the pantheon is special, and he is one of the core Orishas.

Associated Symbols:

- Divination Circle
- Hand of Orunmila

Associated Colors:

- Yellow
- Green

Associated Food:

- Sweet bread
- Yams

Associated Ebo Sacrifice:

- Mudfish
- Rats
- Fried snails

Associated Number:

- 2

Associated Day:

- Tuesday
- 4th October – The Feast of Francis of Assisi

Obatala

The Orisha of the sky, Obatala, is said to be the guardian of purity and defender of the weak and disabled. He was responsible for creating mortal bodies; Olodumare may have breathed existence into them, but he needed the physical bodies to do so. Otherwise, the essence of mortals would not have had anywhere to go. His primary wife was Yemoja, but it is believed his harem comprised more than 200 consorts, his favorite being Yemowo.

One myth tells us that Olodumare permitted Obatala to create land beneath the sky and in water, but Obatala couldn't finish the job, and Olodumare had to finish it himself. However, other stories say that Obatala did create all land, in addition to mortal bodies. In every version of this myth, Obatala was an original Orisha and a member of the core pantheon.

An association with white is one of his key features. Obatala dresses only in white, and virtually everything associated with him is partly or fully white. He has a favorite staff, made from atori shrub vines and named Opaxoro. The atori shrub is around six feet tall and has medicinal properties, but because it isn't a natural white, Obatala had the staff dyed.

Associated Symbols:

- White crown
- Dove
- Opaxoro

Associated Colors:

- White

Associated Food:

- White rice
- Milk
- Shredded coconut
- White bread
- Eggs

Associated Ebo Sacrifice:

- Snakes
- White hens
- Snails

Associated Number:

- 8

Associated Days:

- Monday
- 24th September – The Feast of Our Lady of Mercy

Yemoja

Yemoja is said to be the Divine Earth Mother, The Mother of All Water, and the patron of oceans, rivers, and lakes. She is also the Mother of every Orisha and is often likened to the Virgin Mary in Christian religions. If all that wasn't enough, she protects women and cleanses sorry, comforting everyone she sees as her children.

Another original Orisha, Yemoja is believed to have come down to the Earth while the world was being shaped. She came down on a long rope with sixteen more Orishas that Olodumare created and helped Obatala create mortal bodies. She was also Obatala's main wife. She is unique among some Orishas in that she can interpret the Odu Ifa in its entirety, using cowrie shells rather than pine nuts to access it.

Depictions usually show Yemoja as a mermaid living in West African, Caribbean, or South American waters. She is strongly associated with lakes, oceans, and rivers, and worship typically happens near bodies of water, like runoffs, wells, streams, creeks, and springs. She is believed to be the Ogun River protector in Nigeria; Yoruba people believe this is her main home. Other diaspora religions also consider her a spirit of wealth and a patron of fishermen and those who survive shipwrecks.

Yemoja comes across as a matronly woman when she is in her role of protecting women, specifically pregnant ones. This image of her can be compared to Earth Mother archetypes in different religions, including:

- **Celtic Mythology** – the Morrigan
- **Chinese Mythology** – The Queen Mother of the West
- **Christianity** – the Virgin Mary
- **Egyptian Mythology** – Isis
- **Hinduism** – Parvati and Durga
- **Roman Mythology** – Terra

Associated Symbols:

- Sea stones
- Mermaid
- Shells

Associated Colors:

- Light blue
- White
- Crystal

Associated Food:

- Lelé

- Bitter kola nuts
- Obi
- White corn
- Onion
- Rice

Associated Ebo Sacrifice:

- Jewelry
- Perfume
- White roses
- Blue flowers
- Dishes made from fish or duck

Associated Number:

- 7

Associated Days:

- Sunday
- 2nd February
- 7th September
- Summer Solstice dates

Nana Buluku

She is believed to have been heavily involved in creation, birthing the moon and the sun. Before this, Nana Buluku was the Great Mother, but she retired once the moon and sun had been born, giving other Orishas a chance. Depictions usually show Nana Buluku as an elderly crone, and she is part of the Triple Goddess trinity with Oya Nla and Yemoja. The trinity includes female deity aspects such as the Maiden, Mother, and Crone.

Nana Buluku's children are Lisa – the sun – and Mawu – the moon. However, some myths tell us she is also responsible for all the stars we see in the sky at night. She was an original Orisha, present when the universe was created and helping to shape the world. She is highly regarded among most diaspora religions and is one of the most important pantheon members.

Some myths say that Nana Buluku created perfect deities, but her children were only able to create imperfect ones. It is said that this is why good and evil exist. While Lisa and Mawu were pure, the embodiment of goodness, they couldn't maintain it in what they created, bringing about negativity. However, diaspora religions revere both mother and children.

Associated Symbols:

- Moon
- Sun
- Stars

- Broom shaped like a hook
- Mud
- Triangle

Associated Colors:

- Purple
- Blue
- White

Associated Food:

- Coffee beans
- Coconut
- Rum

Associated Ebo Sacrifice:

- Handkerchief – purple or blue
- Clay vase

Associated Number:

- 7

Associated Days:

- Sunday
- 27th September – the Feast of Our Lady, Star of the Sea

Iya Nla

An original Orisha, Iya Nla is thought to have been the Orisha to provide the power for creation. This puts her on the same level as Olodumare, possibly as his mate or Mother. Creating the universe required energy, and because Iya Nla provided this, she has been known as the Great Mother or the Mother of All Things.

Associated Symbols:

- Tree of Life
- Wellsprings

Associated Colors:

- White
- Gold

Associated Food:

- Fruits, particularly berries and pomegranates
- Beans
- Nuts

Associated Ebo Sacrifice:

- Small game
- Anything from nature, such as herbs, flowers, bark, etc.

Associated Number:

- 1

Associated Day:

- Monday
- 1ˢᵗ September to 4ᵗʰ October – the Creation Season

Osanyin

The patron of all herbalists, Osanyin is sometimes depicted with all his limbs, while others show him with one leg, arm, and eye. He is of the belief that he created every healing herb, and herbalists ask for his help in healing injuries and sickness. His wand is a leaf, and he uses a knife – the leaf and knife illustrate nature's good and bad aspects.

One myth tells us that Osanyin and Orunmila went to war against each other, with Osanyin looking to usurp Orunmila's position in the pantheon. Orunmila fought back by calling a vicious lightning storm down onto Shango's palace, which is where Osanyin was staying. Shango was killed and deified, joining the Orishas, while Osanyin was left maimed. This is why some depictions show him with only one of each limb.

Associated Symbols:

- Birds

- Trees
- Leaves

Associated Colors:

- Yellow
- Green
- Brown

Associated Food:

- Gin
- Corn meal

Associated Ebo Sacrifices:

- 16 green and yellow beads
- 16 healing herbs
- 16 birds

Associated Number:

- 16

Associated Days:

- Wednesday
- 19th March – the Feast of St. Joseph
- 29th September – the Feast of St. Raphael the Archangel

Oshumare

The patron of rainbows, Oshumare is associated with permanence, prosperity, and wealth. Some myths say that our current endeavors will soon reap good fortune when we see a rainbow and pray to the Orisha. Some practitioners also say a connection exists between Oshumare and the mythical pot of gold where a rainbow touches the ground.

He is depicted as snake-like, reflecting a rainbow arcing through the sky in the shape of a slithering snake. According to the Yoruba, a rainbow is Oshumare traveling across the sky, and they use the word "oshumare" to mean rainbow.

Associated Symbols:

- Snake
- Rainbow

Associated Colors:

- Red
- Orange
- Yellow
- Green
- Blue

- Indigo
- Violet
- Any other color associated with a rainbow

Associated Food:

- Mango
- Coconut
- Pineapple
- Banana

Associated Ebo Sacrifice:

- Ceramic items – rainbow colors
- Snakes

Associated Number:

- 4

Associated Days:

- Thursday
- 17th March – the Feast of St. Patrick

Otin

The patron of the Otin River, Otin started as a mortal. During that time, she went from Otan, her home, to a town called Inisa to help protect them from attack by a neighboring town. She was at the forefront of the battle, leading the defenders and fighting on the frontline, successfully using her fearsome spear to repel the attack. She was deified on her death and became the protector of the Otin River.

Associated Symbols:

- River
- Spear

Associated Colors:

- Orange
- Blue

Associated Food:

- Baked beans
- Kola nuts

Associated Ebo Sacrifice:

- Denticle herring
- Butter catfish
- Any other fish found in the Otin River

Associated Number:

- 11

Associated Days:

- Friday

- 30th May – the Feast of St. Joan of Arc

Ori

The Orisha of consciousness and destiny, Ori personifies the concept of essence that every mortal has in their head. This includes the destiny they were given at birth and their consciousness. It is said that when people find balance in themselves, they can ask Ori for help understanding their fate and becoming more self-aware.

Associated Symbols:

- Nkrabea – Adinkra symbol representing the idea of a foretold future

Associated Colors:

- Yellow
- Red

Associated Food:

- Ekuru
- Fried rice
- Goat meat

Associated Ebo Sacrifice:

- Water that a Babalawo has blessed and in a basin

Associated Number:

- 42

Associated Days:

- Monday
- 13th February – the Feast of St. Agabus

Oshosi

The Orisha of meals, beauty, art appreciation, and contemplation, Oshoshi is associated with wealth, hunting, forests, and animals. He can often be seen depicted with a bow and arrow. Although he is a hunter, Oshosi will only kill if necessary, never for sport, and remains highly conscious of the spirit of every animal he slays. This aspect of him revolves around lightness, astuteness, craftiness, and wisdom; throughout, he encourages good energy and positivity.

Associated Symbols:

- Bow and arrow

Associated Colors:

- Breen
- Blue

Associated Food:

- Roast cowpeas
- Black beans
- Axoxô
- Yams

Associated Ebo Sacrifice:

- Guinea fowl
- Goat
- Cooked pig/boar

Associated Numbers:

- 3
- 4
- 7

Associated Days:

- Thursday
- 20th January – the Feast of St. Sebastian
- 6th June – the Feast of St Norbert of Xanten
- 3rd November – the Feast of St Hubert

Oshun

The Orisha of fertility, love, and prosperity, Oshun is also associated with divinity, sensuality, beauty, and femininity. When she became Shango's wife, it raised her importance level in the pantheon. Both the Osun State and Osun River in Nigeria were named to honor her, and she is deeply involved in destiny and divination.

Associated Symbols:

- Gold
- Mint
- Rooster

Associated Colors:

- White
- Yellow
- Coral
- Gold

Associated Food:

- Pepper soup
- Ofe Akwu
- Beef stew

Associated Ebo Sacrifice:

- Sunflowers
- Honey
- Folha-de-dez-reiz
- Mint leaf

Associated Number:

- 5

Associates Days:

- Friday
- 8th September – Feast of the Nativity of the Blessed Virgin Mary

Olokun

Olukun is the patron of the seas and Orisha of all water. Olukun is gender-fluid, switching between female, male, and androgynous. They have an influence over their practitioners' financial prosperity, vitality, and health. The hinterland regions in West Africa revere Olukun as female, while the coastal regions revere them as male. Olukun is androgynous in Santería.

The Yoruba people believe that Olukun was Oduduwa's first wife when he was mortal; after a fight between Olukun and all of Oduduwa's other wives, it is said that the Atlantic Ocean was created. Some traditions state that Olukun lost their temper with mortals and tried drowning all of humanity; they only stopped when they were chained to the bottom of the ocean by Obatala, leaving them forever.

Associated Symbols:

- Coral crown
- Merman or Mermaid
- Sea life

Associated Colors:

- Coral
- Aquamarine
- Blue

Associated Food:

- Melons
- Grains
- Molasses

Associated Ebo Sacrifice:

- Seashells
- Cowrie shells
- Ducks
- Fish

Associated Numbers:

- 7
- 9

Associated Days:

- Sunday
- 30th April – the Feast of St. Adjutor

Chapter 4:

The Hot Orishas

Also called the gbigbona, these Orishas have a hot temper, and their characteristics are impatience, they anger easily, and are brash. Their colors are typically black and red, and they can be vengeful, overzealous tricksters.

Eshu

The Orishas' messenger, Eshu is also the patron of justice and law enforcement. His associations are doorways, transformation, and crossroads, and he can also be a trickster – the embodiment of the gbigbona's contradictory nature. This is also evident in Eshu being a protective guardian and a conniving swindler after knowledge. He seeks the balance between two extremes – happiness and sorrow, justice and injustice, good and bad.

Associated Symbols:

- Sealed scroll

- Scale
- Lion
- Chains

Associated Colors:

- Black
- Red
- Dark blue

Associated Foods:

- Corn
- Rice
- Fish

Associated Ebo Sacrifice:

- Rum
- Palm oil
- Coconut
- Cigars
- Chicken
- Candy

Associated Number:

- 3

Associated Days:

- Wednesday

- 13th June – the Feast of St. Anthony of Padua

Babalu-Aye

A spirit of the Earth, Babalu-Aye is associated with infectious disease and healing. On the one hand, he is said to help people with serious diseases and illnesses recover, particularly when they are near death, but others say he heaps disease upon humanity. We can see this duality in the expression of his powers. He has the ability to warm the body to a temperature that causes a fever, thus burning disease off, but this temperature also has the potential to kill a person.

Associated Symbols:

- Healer's staff
- Sun

Associated Colors:

- Purple
- Yellow
- Brown

Associated Foods:

- Black beans
- Roasted corn

- Rum

Associated Ebo Sacrifice:

- Rum
- Beans
- Black-eyed peas
- Burlap
- Corn
- Tobacco

Associated Number:

- 17

Associated Days:

- Saturday
- 17th December – the Feast of St Lazarus

Shango

Best known as being the Orisha of lightning and thunder, Shango is also related to war, fire, foundations, and virility. He carries a two-bladed axe named O□è, and the Yoruba people consider him a direct ancestor. This is because he was the emperor – the third Alaafin – of the Oyo Empire.

Associated Symbols:

- Brass crown
- Lightning bolt

Associated Colors:

- White
- Red

Associated Food:

- Amalá – a stew made of okra, palm oil, and shrimp

Associated Ebo Sacrifice:

- Cloth – red with white squares
- Thunderstones
- God necklaces – white and red beads, alternating in groups of four or six

Associated Numbers:

- 4
- 6

Associated Days:

- Friday
- 4th December – the Feast of St. Barbara
- 30th September – the Feast of St. Jerome

Ogun

The Orisha of warriors and metallurgy, Ogun's traits include strength, transformation, and healing. Myth tells us that Ogun gave the Orishas access to the Earth by using his dog and metal axe to clear a path for them. Other tales say that he attempted to wrest power from them – including Oduduwa and Obatala – but they stopped him and exiled him.

Associated Symbols:

- Anvils
- Blacksmith tools
- Iron
- Palm fronds
- Dogs

Associated Colors:

- Green
- Black

Associated Food:

- Palm wine
- Meat
- Kola nuts

Associated Ebo Sacrifices:

- Plantains
- Iron nails
- Red meat
- Pomegranate
- Rum
- Cigars

Associated Numbers:

- 3
- 7

Associated Days:

- Wednesday
- 23rd November – St. Clement's Day

Oya

The Orisha of violent storms and wind, Oya is also connected to transformation, rebirth, death, and lightning. She also protects the dead, is the patron of the Niger River, and is Shango's third wife. She is a warrior and is said to have no peers and can defeat anyone who throws down a challenge to her. She protects the spirits of those who have died as they travel to the afterlife and watches over the tombs and cemeteries where their physical bodies lay.

Associated Symbols:

- Whisk
- Lightning bolt
- Copper crown
- Lightning bolt

Associated Colors:

- Burgundy
- Purple
- Red

Associated Food:

- Àkàrà – a fritter made from black-eyed peas or cowpeas

Associated Ebo Sacrifice:

- Machete
- Copper sword
- Red palm oil

Associated Number:

- 9

Associated Days:

- Thursday
- 14th/15th August – the Feast of Our Lady Candelaria

Oduduwa

Originally one of the divine kings, Oduduwa ruled from Ile-Ife. He was also said to have begotten many of the royal Yoruba dynasties, and many rulers could trace back to him as one of their ancestors. Oduduwa is worshipped as a warrior, leader, hero, and the Great Father to the Yoruba people; he was given a praise name for this purpose – Olofin Adimula Oodua.

He was deified on his death and became one aspect of the Orisha he shared a name with. Oduduwa's original version and Obatala were linked, with Oduduwa being one of Olodumare's first Orishas. He took over Obatala's purpose to create Earth's waters. Some evidence also points to the original Oduduwa being one of Obatala's female counterparts.

Associated Symbols:

- Birds
- Sacred Oba's crown

Associated Colors:

- White
- Gold

Associated Food:

- Bean cakes
- Yams
- Plantains

Associated Ebo Sacrifice:

- Birds
- Bird feathers
- Pineapples
- Melons

Associated Number:

- 7

Associated Days:

- Sunday

The Orisha Shrine

During an Ebo ritual, you may want to connect with the Orishas while praying or offering up sacrifices. You can do this with an Orisha Shrine. However, it is worth noting that shrines are not a requirement for worship in this religion; because the Yoruba religion was unrecognized for a long period, worshippers practiced secretly, hiding their shrines. In the 1990s, Orisha worship became legal, and many practitioners are proud of the fact that they created their shrine before the government recognized the faith and kept them going.

Pros and Cons of Creating an Orisha Shrine

Whether you create a shrine or not is entirely down to you. Some say it is unnecessary; others say you should use one in your Orisha worship. Because there are no written guidelines on practicing Orisha worship, you should consider the following pros and cons when you make your decision:

Pros

- **A Stronger Connection with the Orishas:** creating a shrine can allow you to connect more strongly with the Orishas; by praying and worshipping in the same place consistently, you provide the shrine with spiritual energy, and when you use it for your offerings, it makes them more potent.

- **Your Worship Is More Structured:** Shrines allow for better structure in your worship because your rituals and prayers will all happen at the same location. That way, when you want to venerate the Orishas, you know where you should be.

- **Religious Pride:** a shrine helps you to show you are proud of the Yoruba religion. Creating one requires effort and money, so if you can keep it going successfully, it shows you are devoted to the Orishas.

- **Less Work:** once you have created a basic shrine, you won't have to keep doing it whenever you want to make offerings or pray to the Orishas. You can reuse certain items so they won't need replacing for a few worship sessions.

Cons

- **Not So Many Opportunities:** when creating a shrine, you may find your opportunities to make offerings limited – not all offerings are accepted at all places. The shrine connects you with the Orishas, but they might not accept offerings or prayers you might want to make elsewhere.

- **It Can Be Expensive:** it won't be so bad if you only want to worship one Orisha. However, it could get expensive if you want to worship several Orishas. You won't find everything you want in your home, so you must make specific purchases. You will also need to purchase items every time you make an Ebo sacrifice, which can add up, especially if you do the rituals frequently.

- **Time-Consuming:** aside from how long setting up a shrine takes, it must also be cleansed and maintained regularly. If you don't do this, you could invite negative consequences, and the

Orishas may no longer accept your offerings and prayers if your shrine becomes tainted.

- **Negative Energy:** when your shrine is not cleansed or maintained, your essence can become corrupted. This could lead to malevolent Orishas coming into your life, and you may even fall under the influence of the Ajoguns.

Creating an Orisha Shrine

Every shrine is different, as it will be unique to its creator. However, everyone building one should follow some common steps:

1. **Find the right location.** Your shrine must be easily accessible, where it can't be destroyed or get dirty. It can be inside your house or in a shed or covered area outdoors where the elements can't get at it.
2. **Use a raised platform.** This could be a table, box, dais, or anything similar. Put the platform in your chosen area, preferably against something solid, like a wall. It doesn't want to be too high as you will kneel when using it.
3. **Cover it.** Find a cloth or material that matches the color/s for the Orisha you want to worship.

It must be clean and relatively plain – only checkered patterns, stripes, etc., are acceptable. If the cloth has too much of a pattern or is flowery, it will distract you, and you will struggle to connect with the Orishas.

4. **Use an offering vessel.** Place a bowl, shallow basin, plate, or something similar on your altar; it should be made of a non-alloy metal, clay, wood, or ceramic. Try to choose one made of a material associated with the Orisha you want to worship.

5. **Add candles.** One or more candles should be used, but make sure their colors are those associated with your chosen Orishas. You can purchase single or double-colored candles – these will do just fine.

6. **Use a candleholder.** It should be made from a non-alloy metal and must be sturdy enough to keep your candle upright and in place.

Some Orishas will require specific items. These include:

Obatala:

- Cover your altar with a plain, white cloth, like a cotton tablecloth.

- Use a white candle
- Place a sopera (soup tureen), a metal crown, and a dove-handled bell on your altar
- Add an icon showing Obatala or a statue
- Offer white animals or foods during the Ebo ritual
- Never include alcohol in your offerings – Obatala will be offended

Shango:

- Cover your altar in red cloth with white squares
- Use a red or a white and red double candle
- Add thunderstones, a gold and red crown, and a two-edged sword or axe
- Use an icon or statue of Shango
- Your ritual offerings should include hot, spicy foods, amalá, or red foods

Yemoja:

- Cover your altar with plain blue cloth
- Use a blue candle
- Include seas shells, fans, pearls, a silver and blue crown, and images of mermaids, fish, dolphins, and other sea life

- Add an icon or statue of Yemoja and include blue flowers
- Your offerings should include seafood, silver jewelry, perfume, white wine, or coffee during the Ebo ritual

Oya:

- Cover your altar with plain burgundy or purple cloth
- Use a purple candle
- Include copper jewelry, a copper crown, a lightning bolt representation, and shea butter
- Add a statue or icon of Oya and a bowl filled with water – this represents a river
- Your ritual offering should include red wine, eggplant, beets, purple grapes, or chocolate

Oshosi:

- Cover your altar with plain green or blue cloth
- Use a green or blue candle
- Include a bow and arrows, deer antlers, animal furs, turtle shells, ram horns, or anything else you might obtain when hunting
- Add an icon or statue of Oshosi with his bow and arrow

- Include large or small game meat, fruit, or real feathers as your ritual offerings

Ogun:

- Cover your altar with plain blue, green, or red cloth
- Use a blue, green, or red candle
- Include blacksmith tools, an iron crown, and anything else made of iron
- Add an icon or statue of Ogun using an anvil
- Include pomegranates, red meat, plantains, iron nails, cigars, or rum in your ritual offerings

Orisha Shrine Cleansing and Maintenance

This doesn't take much effort, but it must be done regularly to ensure your shrine remains clean and uncorrupted by negative energy. Try to set some time aside once a week to do your maintenance and cleanse the shrine every couple of months.

Shrine Maintenance

Shrine maintenance is really quite simple; all you need to do is clean your ritual items of any dirt and wash the cloth. You will need to remove any permanent items on your altar and store them away carefully while you clean things.

1. First, remove any debris from your offering vessel or the altar. If you use animals or food, they are bound to leave traces behind, which must all be cleaned up. Use soap and water to clean the vessel and remove wax drips from your candle holders.

2. Next, take everything off your altar and remove the cloth for washing. You can do this in a washing machine or by hand, but it must clean off any stains or dirt that get on there from your rituals. Do NOT damage the cloth while washing it.

3. Next, ensure your altar platform is in good repair and clean. If it needs cleaning, use a natural cleaning solution, and make any repairs that need doing. When your altar is in good order, and your cloth is washed and dried, cover the altar with the cloth again.

4. Lastly, place the offering vessel and other altar objects back on it and, if necessary, replace candles or other supplies. You can do this now or before your next ritual; it's up to you.

Shrine Cleansing

It is critical to cleanse your altar regularly to remove any corrupt or negative energy that might have built up.

You can do this in several ways, but the most common ways are as follows:

Smudging

This requires using incense or herbs to remove bad spirits and negative energy. You will need the following for this:

- Some incense or a bunch of herbs
- An incense holder or a fireproof holder
- A clean cloth

Do the following:

1. Take everything off the altar and store it all somewhere safe
2. Use the cloth to wipe around the altar counter-clockwise. While doing this, visualize bad energy surrounding your alternative and speak your intention to remove it
3. Light the incense or herb bundle and blow or waft the smoke around the altar. This counteracts evil forces or negative energy
4. The herb bundle or incense can be left to burn down, thus applying even more cleansing energy, but do not leave them unattended.
5. Once done, remove the incense or herb bundle and dispose of it safely. Then place everything back on your altar.

Using a Holy Water or Floral Spritz

This will require the following items:

- A spray bottle
- Holy water or floral water

Here's what to do:

1. Fill the spray bottle with your chosen water and place it on your altar.
2. Pray aloud, request a blessing, and speak your intentions aloud
3. Take the spray bottle and spritz the contents over the altar and everything on it. As you do so, pray to your chosen Orisha
4. Leave the altar for 15 minutes – say cleansing prayers or meditate while you wait
5. Spray the altar again, then leave it for 15 minutes
6. Do this for a total of five times – around an hour in total – request an altar blessing from your chosen Orisha

Quick Methods

Quicker cleansing methods include the following:

- Blow negative energy from your shrine using a sacred fan or feather wand
- Sweep evil spirits and corruption away using a besom

- Absorb negative energy by placing a bowl of salt or some crystals or ritual stones on the altar
- Use an essential oils diffuser to ward off evil spirits and flood your shrine with positive energy
- Spray the shrine with essential oils or your favorite perfume to remove negative energy
- Say a cleansing prayer and request a blessing from your chosen Orisha to protect you from evil and bring positive energy

Glossary and Essential Phrases

The following are some of the more common words you will come across in this subject:

- **Ajogun:** the evil spirits of Ifa and the Orishas' counterparts
- **Așẹ:** energy permeating everything, living or nonliving. Așẹ is one of the most important parts of the Ifa belief system and has mostly a spiritual purpose
- **Ayé:** what the Yoruba people call Earth and the physical world
- **Dafa:** a particular Ifa ritual using the Ikin Ifa
- **Ebo:** a ritual where sacrificial offerings are made to the Orishas to appease them and gain their favor
- **Egun:** the spirits of ancestors that the Yoruba people and some diaspora religions worship
- **Ifa:** The Yoruba people's religion

- **Ikin Ifa:** cowrie shells or kola nuts used in Ifa divination; practitioners cast and interpret them to read the Odu Ifa
- **Ile-Ife:** The Yoruba people's holy city, an important place for religious worship.
- **Iponri:** the destiny or divine consciousness sought by humans through Ifa rituals
- **Iroke Ifa:** tools used just before divination rituals to tap on the Opon Ifa to gain the attention of the Orishas
- **Irukere:** a tool similar to a brush used during rituals to ward off negative energy or evil spirits
- **Loas:** higher spirits that Voodoo practitioners' worship. These are more involved with humanity on a personal level than the Orishas, but in many cases, each Loa equates to a particular Orisha
- **Odu Ifa:** knowledge gathered by Ifa priestesses and priests. It is used during divination rituals to help a person determine their destiny
- **Odu:** the 256 chapters in the Odu Ifa
- **Olodumare:** the Supreme Being responsible for creating the universe
- **Olofi:** another of Olodumare's aspects, responsible for overseeing Earth

- **Olorun:** one of Olodumare's aspects, responsible for overseeing the heavens
- **Opele Ifa:** divine chain used in Ifa rituals
- **Opon Ifa:** sacred trays used in Ifa rituals
- **Ori:** the essence contained inside the head of every living being, sometimes called their soul
- **Orishas:** the divine beings the Yoruba people worship; also worshipped by other diaspora religions. They are much like the Catholic saints or angels and syncretized with Santerían saints or angels.
- **Orún:** the spiritual realm where the egun, Orishas, iponri, and Olodumare reside; sometimes called the heavens
- **Santería:** another religion that the Yoruba people's descendants developed in the 19th century in Cuba. It combines three religions – Spiritism, Catholicism, and Ifa
- **Voodoo:** a term that covers multiple versions of the religion people from the Americas and the Caribbean practice

Essential Phrases

Lastly, as a bit of fun, if you ever find yourself in Nigeria in the presence of Yoruba people, you might want to learn a few phrases so you can talk to them:

WORD/ PHRASE	YORUBA	EXPLANATION
Hello	Ẹ n lẹ (en-le)	The Yoruba people are very traditional, especially where greetings are concerned – they consider it one of the most important aspects of their culture, particularly when talking to their elders. Women traditionally kneel when greeting someone, while men lay on the ground face-down
Thank You	E se/o se	Yoruba people from central and north-west Nigeria firmly believe in etiquette and good manners. If you say 'thank you' to them in their dialect, it will earn you a few brownie points. E se is used when talking to an older person, while o se is less formal and used when talking to people of your own age or your friends.
Yes/No	Bẹẹ ni/ra ra:	If a Yoruba person asks if you are a tourist, you should respond with one of these, depending on your answer.

Where is the bathroom?	Nibo ni baluwẹ wa	It's frustrating if you need to use the bathroom, but no one understands when you speak! If you are in the company of Yoruba people, you can use this phrase.
Turn Left/ Turn Right	Ya sowo otun (ya-so-wo-o-tun)/ya si apa osi (ya-see-apa-oh-see)	If you are lost and ask for directions, you can understand them by learning these two
Stop here	Duro (du-ro)	If you use taxis, you will often need to let the driver know where you need to get out. Using this phrase will ensure you get out in the right place
Delicious	O dun	Yoruba people make some of the most delicious, spicy food, and if you partake of one of their meals, you might want to tell them what you thought of it. This phrase will go down well with your hosts

I'm hungry	Ebi n pa mi (a-bi-pa-me)	We all need to eat, and you must learn how to get food in the Yoruba areas. Using this phrase will ensure someone directs you to where you can eat
Water	Omi (Oh-me)	It gets very hot in Nigeria, and water is essential, so learn this word to get some life-giving water
How much is this?	Eelo ni eleyi?	Nigerian markets are not the easiest places for tourists to navigate, and learning a few Yoruba phrases will help you get the best deal. Start by asking how much something is
Too expensive	Gb'owo l'ori (Bo-wo-lo-ri)	The item might be out of your reach money-wise, so tell the seller you think it's too expensive.
Beautiful/ Handsome	lẹwa/arewa Okurun	Nigerians are friendly people and often throw out compliments while talking to people. Knowing a few could definitely help you make some new friends

Let's get a drink	Jẹ ka mu nkan	After a long day of sightseeing and shopping, you might want to get a drink with some new friends. This is how you suggest it
I miss you	Aro re so mi	We all want to know that we have been missed so learn how to tell someone that you missed them
How are you?	Bawo ni	Nigerians will say this to you when asking about your well-being, so learn it and ask your new Nigerian friends the same – they will appreciate it
Call the police	Pe awọn ọlọpaa	If an emergency arises, use this phrase to get someone to call the police for you
No problem	Kosi wahala (Ko-see-wa-ha-la)	This is the Nigerian/ Yoruba equivalent of no worries, or Hakuna Matata, as it is in Swahili
Excuse me	jọwọ	If you need to get the attention of someone, use this phrase

See you tomorrow	Emi yoo ri ọ ni ọla	This is how to tell a friend that you will get together the next day
My name is	Orukọ mi ni	This is a simple way of introducing yourself; simply add your name at the end

Numbers – 1 to 10

- **1** – ikan
- **2** – meji
- **3** – meta
- **4** – merin
- **5** – marun
- **6** – mefa
- **7** – meje
- **8** – mejo
- **9** – mesan
- **10** – mewa

Conclusion

The Yoruba religion has enjoyed a long but mysterious history. Having read this guide, I hope you understand more about it and why Yoruba practitioners keep their secrets closely guarded. They don't want their beliefs and rituals to become twisted by those who don't care about or understand them and just want to use them for their own end, whether it matches the original beliefs or not. All they ask is that you respect their beliefs and rituals – not too much to request, is it?

The Ifa divination system is an important aspect of Yoruba spiritual practice, and two of the most important concepts are seeking higher planes of consciousness and fate. Everyone on this planet came from Olodumare, so it makes sense that we will all return to him one day. The Yoruba people live by the tenet that our time in life is meant to focus on determining our destinies and getting our ori ready to reunite with its iponri. Once the reunion has taken place and the spirit is whole once more, we can understand the scale of our achievements.

The Orishas are also considered incredibly important, and virtually all aspects of life on Earth are connected to them. Reverence for the Orishas dictates everything we do, all we eat, our actions, and how we behave. None of us should be surprised by this, given that the ori is said to be the essence of an Orisha inside our heads. Now that you've come to the end of this guide, it's time to figure out which Orisha belongs to you. Use this guide as a stepping-stone, a starting point to learning more about the Orisha and how they might influence your life.

Good luck with your journey.

References

Mark, Joshua J. "Orisha." *World History Encyclopedia*, www.worldhistory.org/Orisha/#:~:text=Orisha%20 (also%20given%20as%20Orisa.

"Orisha: The 12 Most Powerful Gods from Yoruba Mythology." *Www.santuariolunar.com*, 3 Mar. 2022, www.santuariolunar.com/orisha-gods-and-goddesses/.

"The 5 Most Influential Orishas." *The Guardian Nigeria News - Nigeria and World News*, 11 Aug. 2019, guardian.ng/life/the-5-most-influential-orishas/.

"Yoruba - Introduction, Location, Language, Folklore, Religion, Major Holidays, Rites of Passage." *Everyculture. com*, 2009, www.everyculture.com/wc/Mauritania-to-Nigeria/Yoruba.html.

"Yoruba Gods That Influence Lives | FunTimes Magazine." *Www.funtimesmagazine.com*, www. funtimesmagazine.com/2022/10/08/414420/

yoruba-gods-that-influence-lives#:~:text=Yoruba%20 mythology%20teaches%20that%20there.

"Yoruba Mythology: Female Orishas and Their Roles." *The Guardian Nigeria News - Nigeria and World News*, 30 Oct. 2022, guardian.ng/life/ yoruba-mythology-female-orishas-and-their-roles/.

"Yoruba Mythology: The Orishas of the Yoruba Race." *The Guardian Nigeria News - Nigeria and World News*, 25 Sept. 2022, guardian.ng/life/ yoruba-mythology-the-orishas-of-the-yoruba-race/.